THE ABC GUIDE TO
MINECRAFT

TIPS, TRICKS, HINTS AND CHEATS

FOR THE ULTIMATE MINECRAFT EXPERIENCE!

By Paul Adams

THE ABC GUIDE TO
MINECRAFT

TIPS, TRICKS, HINTS AND CHEATS

FOR THE ULTIMATE MINECRAFT EXPERIENCE!

An imprint of Gauthier Publications
St. Clair Shores, MI 48236

Gauthier Publications
P.O. Box 806241
Saint Clair Shores, MI 48080
Attention Permissions Department

The images used in the book are property of Majong and have no affiliation
with Gauthier Publications. This is an unofficial guidebook and is not in
anyway associated with Minecraft the game or any editions of Minecaft

Book Design: Elizabeth Gauthier
Font Design for Mincraft Font: MadPixel

1st Edition
Gauthier Publications
www.EATaBOOK.com

ISBN: 978-0615949543

FOR ALL THOSE WHO LOVE MINECRAFT

About Minecraft PE

    Minecraft Pocket Edition is the Android and iPhone client for the popular PC and Xbox game. It's all about creating – just about anything you can think of, with more possibilities appearing with every update to the game. Players build homes, grow food, farm livestock, explore caves, mine ore and much, much more.

    While the PC version of Minecraft is certainly the freshest choice with the most recent updates, items and extras, sometimes you just have to get your Minecraft on while away from your home computer. That's what Minecraft PE is all about. It's no secret the game can prove pretty addicting for some, as the sheer number of choices and different things to do put boredom to bed.

For experienced players of the original version, Minecraft Pocket Edition presents a fun new way to play an old favorite. For new players just getting to the game though, there are many things they must learn if they want to survive even their first night. By following the tips and points in this guide, even veteran players may be able to glean some new knowledge which will improve their Minecraft Pocket Edition game play experience.

Building a Base

When just starting out in Minecraft PE, players will find themselves in the middle of nowhere, with nothing to get between them and all the nasty things that want to kill them. Building an adequate shelter should be the first priority for any Minecraft player. It doesn't need to be anything fancy or complicated, just solid and with a door barring any points of ingress or egress.

Homes can be made from practically anything, including the dirt and grass under your feet. Many of the fixtures inside a home will require wood though, so it's a good point to find some trees and start punching them as soon as you begin a new game. Wood logs can be broken down into planks, then sticks, then used to craft just about every useful tool in the game.

Every home should have a bed, which sets a player's spawn point when they sleep in it. Putting a bed in your home is the only way to really make it your "home", so finding some sheep and gathering wool is a good next step. Homes also typically include crafting tables, furnaces and other useful blocks, along with lighting and whatever else the player desires.

Just because your home doesn't need to be large and elaborate doesn't also mean you can't make it so if you wish. Some players spend days or even weeks working on their dream homes, getting everything down to the last, meticulous detail. Because Minecraft is the kind of sandbox style game where players can do anything they desire, it's only natural that some would spend lots of time building.

CRAFTING TABLES

Crafting Tables are every Minecraft player's best friend. They are the key to making many of the more advances goods, tools, fixtures and other items players will need to survive their stay in Minecraft PE. A single log of wood may be broken down into four planks, which can then be arranged to create one of these tables. Besides planks, sticks and some dyes, crafting tables are one of the few items players can create without using a crafting table.

Every home should have one or two of these in it and every player should always carry one around in his or her inventory. You never know when you're going to need to build something on the fly and being able to do it while you're in a field, cave or elsewhere, instead of going back home to craft, can save much time and frustration.

If you find yourself far from home, without a table

and facing a sudden need to craft, don't panic. If there are any trees nearby, a single log will solve your problems. If you're underground, you may be able to find wooden planks if you can gain access to an abandoned mineshaft. Fences and planks are frequently found in these places, being used to support the stone above.

      Crafting tables are necessary for making furnaces, doors, glass panes, stairs and many other items needed in home construction. Because of this, your first task after finding some wood should be to make one of these babies. Crafting tables do stack, so you can carry a bunch of them with you and place them as needed, giving yourself a wide area in which you can create items.

DIGGING

Much of Minecraft PE comes down to digging. Digging can be done with bare hands, but players will find themselves pretty frustrated if they're dealing with anything besides dirt. Picks are useful for breaking through stone and harder stuff, while shovels are better for dealing with dirt, gravel and sand – softer stuff in general. Using either of these tools to try and collect the wrong kind of blocks will result in longer work times and the possibility that whatever block you break will disappear rather than make its way to your inventory.

One of the biggest mistakes new players to Minecraft PE make is to dig a hole straight down. Sure, this is a good way to get to the bottom of the world quickly, but it's also an excellent way for players to find themselves dug into a deep ravine and dead from a long fall. More often than not, hazards like empty space, lava and enemies will be waiting to claim the life of a player who digs straight down. Digging one block forward and two blocks down will create a kind of staircase which means safer spelunking for you and an easier return trip when you're done. It is a much better option than digging straight down and significantly less likely to cause your death.

Tools used for digging come in a variety of materials, from lowly wood up to tough and durable diamond. It should be noted that though gold tools suffer a relatively short life, they do outperform even diamond tools in terms of speedy mining or digging. Because iron tools should suffice for mining everything players need, there's actually little reason to waste diamonds on shovels or picks just yet. They are much better used in making armor or weapons.

Evening Falls...

When you first spawn in Minecraft PE, you'll find yourself facing bright skies and a sunny day, unless it's raining of course. Enemies don't spawn in the sunlight, or within 14 blocks of a torch, so all that light means you should have an easy time collecting your first materials and making a place to live. You better do that too, because when evening falls, all those baddies that stayed away during the day come out to play.

Night in Minecraft is a bad time to find yourself outside without shelter, so hopefully you've built up a place to live before your first evening. If you haven't, don't panic just yet. It's possible to make it through the night without a home, but not so easy to do it with style.

Players who find themselves in the middle of nowhere when night comes can still survive. Digging three blocks down and then placing a block to cover the hole above your head will put you into a cramped space, but it will keep you safe from enemies all the same. Sitting in that dark hole, you can wait until morning comes.

The sun damages some monsters, like zombies and skeletons, which sends them fleeing for the nearest body of water or source of overhead cover. Some enemies, like spiders, will not die when the sun comes up. However, they do stop being hostile, which means you can walk around them and avoid a fight.

Finding Diamonds

One of the main goals for most Minecraft PE players is finding diamonds in their world. Diamonds are used to make a variety of items, like armor, weapons, tools and even the nether reactor. Because diamonds can be used to create so many different things, players will need to find lots of diamonds if they plan on getting the most out of their game. Digging for diamonds isn't like looking for coal or iron – you have to dig down deep.

The best way to find diamonds is to start your search at Y: 11. That's the height at which most diamonds naturally spawn when generating a world. It's also the height at which the majority of lava pools in a world exist, so special care must be taken when looking for diamonds. You will want to bring along a bucket of water to deal with any lava spills, which can otherwise prove fatal in a few seconds.

It is possible to find diamonds in other ways than mining them out of the earth yourself. If you manage to find an NPC village with a blacksmith, be sure to check out the chest inside. These chests typically contain armor, metals and saplings, along with the occasional food items and yes, diamonds. This isn't as reliable as digging down to the proper height and going through the dirt and stone yourself.

Another way to find diamonds outside of the ground is getting them out of temples. Temples can spawn in jungle and desert biomes, with both temple types being distinctly different from one another. Desert temples include long falls and TNT traps, while jungle temples have many tripwires and dispensers set up to fire arrows. Both structures are generally hazardous and both have a good chance of containing several diamonds. It's also possible to walk away with all those useful traps, if you're careful enough to get them out without getting got yourself.

GENERATING WORLDS

One of the best parts about Minecraft Pocket Edition is the random world generation feature. When creating a world, players can allow the game to make up something completely random for them. This could result in spawning with a village nearby, or on a deserted island in the middle of nowhere.

Experimenting with this random generation and trying to find the best possible world before you start playing is a good way to get the most from your gaming time.

While this random generation is fine for most players, others will want to get something good the first time, without trying over and over to get a great, random world. This is where Minecraft's unique seed system comes in. Players can generate pre-defined worlds using seeds which the game produces at a request. When making a world, entering a specific seed into the generator will create a specific world. This is a great way for map makers to share their worlds with other players. The current best seeds are always changing as updates are released and new features are added to the game. This means that some seeds which are good now may not be so good later, as the actual makeup of the world changes with the addition of new block types. There are too many seed tracking websites to list them all here, so finding sources for seeds shouldn't take more than a minute if you really want them.

If you find yourself in a unique world that really stands out from others you've seen, or if you've gone through a lot of work to develop land and want other players out there to experience your creations, getting a seed to share with others is something you might want to do.

Amassing wealth through mining, fighting and other tasks just happens naturally in Minecraft PE. Items which aren't immediately used can likely be used at some point in play to make something useful to the player. This means lots of stuff ends up in chests, which are great for holding loot and keeping your inventory free and clear to grab up more stuff. While enemies don't raid homes for loot, home security is still an issue to address in Minecraft.

Creepers are some of the most annoying creatures video gaming has ever seen. They literally creep up on a player, hiss and then explode, destroying everything in a small radius. Protecting your home from their interference is easy enough with lights everywhere, but that's a very high maintenance solution to an ever-present problem. There are simpler ways to deal with these menaces.

Building two block wide, four block deep moats around your home should be enough to keep most baddies out. Filling them with lava or lining the bottom with sand and loading the pits with cactus blocks are both great ways to kill the things trying to kill you. Both of these security systems destroy all the drops from mobs though, so they do come with an inherent cost. Water is less effective at keeping out creepers and other nuisances, but there is one saving grace for it.

Explosions which occur underwater do not damage nearby blocks. While a submerged creeper will still damage *you* if you are close enough, it won't even scratch your home or the nearby land. This makes water sound like the best option among the three, but there's something more to it. Every monster in the game (except slimes) will float at the top of water, trying to jump out onto solid land at the soonest possible moment. Many creepers in water still manage to hop out right when they explode, effectively beating this home security system.

Iron's Many Uses

While many Minecraft PE players will be in a frantic search to find diamonds as fast as possible, it turns out that iron is actually one of the most useful ores in the game. Once mined and smelted at a furnace, iron can be converted into a handful of effective items which make Minecraft easier for the player. Iron is good for tools and weapons, as well as armor. It can also be used to make solid doors which don't operate like their wooden counterparts.

With the 0.8 update to Minecraft PE, mine carts and rails were both added to the game. These make transportation over long distances a breeze by speeding up movement and getting the player there faster. These items also take iron to build – lots of iron, in fact. Most players will go through several stacks of iron before they find their first diamonds, so it's not a metal to ignore.

Perhaps one of the best uses for iron is in creating an iron golem. These big, hulking behemoths really put the hurt on anything hostile that happens to wander too close to you. While they make great sentries for keeping your base safe, they do tend to wander off if you don't keep them boxed into an area. Make sure to put up plenty of fences or other walls before crafting these things, or you could be out lots of resources for nothing. Iron golems require 36 iron total, so they sure aren't cheap to make.

Jumping (and Falling)

Jumping is something you'll be doing a lot in Minecraft Pocket Edition. Hopping over small gaps while running will help you to keep running and not get caught up on the ground. Jumping from great heights into water sources will allow you to get back to ground level more or less immediately, without damaging yourself at all. Jumping between trees in jungle biomes is also a possibility, thanks to the vines which tend to grow on them.

When you're running, the maximum distance you can cross in a single leap is around 3.5 blocks. This means that land 4 blocks or more away will be just out of reach, even for those jumpers who get a running start. This is still enough distance to cross over big holes in the ground, as well as deep and jagged ravines in the earth. Jumping won't get you everywhere, but with the right timing and some forethought, it will get you to most places.

Unless it is mitigated with something like water, vines or a ladder, fall damage will kill a player who takes enough tumbles. A player can fall up to 3 blocks without getting hurt, so if you have a long distance drop with nothing safe on the bottom, you can try to crawl down several blocks at a time. There's a way to do all the falling you want without having to worry about this though.

If you bring a water bucket along with you, you can put the source block of water down at the edge of a drop and let the water tumble downward. Grab the source back up in your bucket, then jump into the stream. It will disappear, but it will also stop you from dropping so fast that you get hurt. Alternatively, you can leave the water to act as a kind of ladder for your later return trip. Be aware, mobs can also climb these "water ladders".

KILLING FOES

When traps and tricks won't keep enemies away from you, it's time to draw steel and strike them down. Swords are the best items for dealing direct damage to mobs and getting rid of them. Like the tools you use to cultivate land and create a home, swords also come in wood, stone, iron, gold and diamond varieties. It should be noted that gold swords are especially flimsy, doing as much damage as wood and lasting about as long. Using gold for weapons and armor is a big waste.

All swords are made with two items; a single stick and two pieces of wood, stone or ore. This means they require a crafting table to make. If you're carrying one with you, you can replace your weapon with ease when it breaks. While swords will do the most damage to enemies, you can still kill them with other items. Axes come in at a close second and make a good replacement for a sword in a pinch. If your weapon breaks and you can't replace it, don't be afraid to fall back on your tools.

Zombies move slowly and are relatively easy to kill. They can be dangerous if they manage to pick up a weapon though. Skeletons are easy to beat; instead of going to them and getting full of arrows, build a two block high wall and hide behind it, making them come to you. Spiders can hop and climb walls, so they're kind of bothersome. They can climb straight up, but not horizontally across a ceiling, so you may build a ridge along the walls of your base to effectively keep spiders out altogether. Creepers are best avoided but can be killed by running and striking, thus knocking them back and stopping them from exploding you.

Cave spiders are especially bad because they poison the player upon contact, unlike the surface dwelling spiders which just jump into a person. This poison won't kill you, but it will take you down to as little as 1 health (1 half heart), which will make it pretty easy for *anything else* to kill you. If you plan on digging around in abandoned mineshafts, bring along a bucket of milk or two, since the stuff is the only cure for poison in the game.

Livestock

Cows, chickens, sheep and pigs are all livestock available in Minecraft and Minecraft PE. Cows like wheat and can be killed for beef and leather, or milked with an empty bucket an infinite number of times. Sheep also like wheat, but they are only good for wool – no meat at all. Pigs are *only* good for meat and drop no skin, wool or other extra items. Chickens drop meat and feathers when killed. The latter is used in creating arrows. Chickens also lay eggs occasionally when left to wander around.

Breeding livestock is the best way to ensure a steady supply of new animals is always ready for you to eat. Feed two cows (or sheep) wheat and they will make a baby calf (or lamb). Chickens eat the seeds which you can find when breaking grass or harvesting wheat. Pigs are rather picky eaters, even if that doesn't make much sense: they will only eat carrots, which are found as rare drops from zombies or in NPC villages.

To keep your animals from wandering off, you will need to create a pen with some fences. There is a particular glitch in Minecraft which allows animals to glitch through the corner posts in fences, a glitch they often take advantage of to get loose and run away. This glitch is easily defeated by building a wall of solid blocks beneath the fencing. While the corners in the fencing will still be vulnerable, animals won't jump onto the solid blocks beneath to try and break free.

If you don't eat enough food, your hunger meter will run low and you'll start taking damage. Depending on the difficulty you're using, this damage will stop at five hearts (easy) or one heart (normal, hard). It's important to have enough food around, so make sure you breed new animals to replace the ones you kill and eat.

Minecarts

With the 0.8 update, minecarts and rails were introduced to Minecraft PE. These are useful tools for traveling over long distances in a short period of time, especially in single player mode where other players won't be around to break up the tracks. Even if you're playing alone though, mobs can still spawn on and around rails, which is why adequate lighting must be maintained.

Minecarts are made from iron and 5 pieces are necessary to craft one cart. They will not run on land, so don't even think of trying to drive them around like cars. Minecarts will move very slowly if you crawl inside and push forward. To get the most speed out of them, you will need to utilize either descending slopes or powered rail.

Minecarts need a lot of iron to make, so it's a good idea to pick them up and take them with you when you're done with them. They don't stack in your inventory, so you should try to limit the number of minecarts you carry around at any given time to one, two at most. They aren't good for much more than movement right now, but future updates promise to make minecarts as much a part of Minecraft PE as they are in the standard version of the game.

Nether Reactor

Many players who have enjoyed Minecraft on the PC know about the Nether. It's a dark, dangerous place, full of lava and powerful enemies. While there is yet no Nether in the Pocket Edition of the game, there is something similar. The Nether Reactor is a construct unique to Minecraft PE which brings the Nether to the player, rather than taking the player to the Nether.

Be warned, using the Nether Reactor will completely terramorph nearby land, turning it into a hellish space full of zombified pigs. These mobs come with gold swords standard and they know how to use them. Do not use the Nether Reactor in your home, or in someone else's home (unless you really want to screw them over). It's best to find a wide, flat area with nothing around if you want to use this puppy.

The blueprints for the reactor are easy enough to follow. Just by looking at the picture given here, it's clear to see how they are put together. By following this same design, you too can craft a Nether Reactor of your own. They are very useful for getting a lot of experience, gold and other drops in a short amount of time.

The gold blocks required to build a Nether Reactor will take some time to make. Each needs 9 gold ingots and there are four total, so you're going to need 36 pieces of gold to make the base. The reactor core itself requires some gold and diamonds to craft, so you will need still more gold to build a functional reactor.

Online Play

Currently, there is no online play feature for Minecraft PE. Unlike the PC or Xbox versions of the game, where joining a server is as easy as clicking a couple buttons, there are *no* servers for the Pocket Edition of Minecraft. This doesn't mean that you can't still play with other people though. Local area network games allow multiple players to all enjoy the same Minecraft world, but only if they're all physically close to one another.

Hosting a "server" like this is so simple it hurts. You literally need to do nothing. Just being in your world and keeping it open will be enough for other players to join, if and when they get close enough to you to do so. Joining games is easy too, since all you need to do is look at the extremely short list of available games nearby and pick one from among them. There are currently plans to make online play a feature for Minecraft PE, but the current version of the game still doesn't include this feature. Be sure to update regularly if you want the most recent version of Minecraft PE on your phone or other device.

Protecting Yourself

While you're working tirelessly to protect your home and land from outside influences, you can't forget to protect yourself, too. It's all a waste if you end up dead and gearless in a pit somewhere, so don't underestimate the importance of a decent suit of armor.

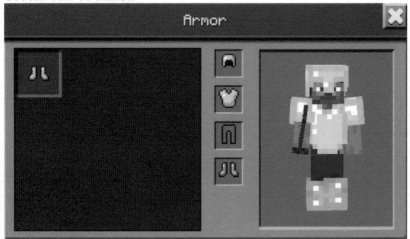

While you may find a few scant pieces of leather on random cows while roaming around, the odds are much better than your first suit of armor will be one of iron. Iron is strong and durable, providing armor with a long life. Iron armor reduces incoming damage by 50%, taking that damage upon itself instead of allowing it to be inflicted on your life. It does eventually break, and there are better materials than iron for guarding your body.

Gold is not one of those materials. While you can technically use gold to make armor and weapons, you shouldn't waste the precious resource on something so silly. Gold armor breaks quickly and does relatively little to stop incoming damage, working about as well as leather armor for taking hits. If you want the best possible protection, you're going to have to find some diamonds somewhere.

Diamond armor is the very best. A full suit will provide you with 10 armor, which will reduce the damage from most mob attacks to a measly 1-2 health. When fighting against weaker monsters, you may take no damage at all. It protects against explosions and environmental hazards like lava, too. For a helmet, chestplate, leggings and boots, you will need 24 diamonds or metal ingots.

Q UESTS?

You may have played lots of online multi player games in the past which were all about questing. Minecraft PE is not one of those games. Because there isn't really any specific goal to meet, some players will get bored with the lack of direction and move on to other games relatively quickly. However, you can give yourself quests to complete instead.

Building a large and impressive home is certainly a feat. Finding abandoned mineshafts, temples and other natural wonders is also something to be proud of. If this all just doesn't do it for you though, you're still in luck. Thanks to the seed system, players can create maps for other players to download, maps with quests and contrived plots already established.

For instance, Hunger Games is an especially popular gameplay mode for Minecraft PE. It pits players against one another in a kill-or-be-killed world where food and tools are scarce. Someone had to make those maps, then generate seeds for those worlds, then make the seeds available for other players to see. It's a lot of work to set it up, but downloading someone else's world and jumping into it yourself doesn't take more than a couple minutes.

If you have a good idea of your own, don't be afraid to build it and make it available to other players. People are always looking for new reasons to appreciate Minecraft PE, and giving them one more will probably go over pretty well.

Rail and Powered Rail

Rail and powered rail are used to travel long distances in Minecraft PE in a relatively short amount of time. By riding a minecart on built rails, it's possible to travel 8 blocks (or more) in the same time it would take you to walk a single one. Anything that can help players to move 8 times faster than normal is something which should be utilized to the fullest extent.

Rail carries minecarts from one point to the next. It requires six iron ingots and a stick to make 16 pieces of rail, so setting up an extensive rail system will naturally take a ton of resources. If you can manage to find any abandoned mineshafts underground, you will also have found an excellent source of rails. There is usually a ton of rail lying in those shafts and you can take it back home with you easily.

Powered rail works like regular rails, but it does a little bit more. It pushes the minecart forward with an incredible burst of speed, but only if it is powered when the minecart travels over it. This can be done with redstone torches, made from torches and redstone. Powered rail is absolutely necessary to push a minecart up the side of a hill, but it also speeds up travel over flat land and descending slopes. Powered rail is made from six gold ingots and a stick, along with a single piece of redstone.

Knowing how to use these two types of rail in tandem is the key to maximizing the movement you get for the resources you spend. Generally, a piece of powered rail every 8-12 blocks will be enough to keep a minecart moving over flat land. Place powered rail every 3-4 blocks when trying to make it up a hill, or else the push from one piece will not be enough to get you to the next. Gold is much harder to find than iron, so use those powered rails as sparingly as possible.

Survival Mode v Creative Mode

When playing Minecraft PE, there are two basic game types to choose from. In survival mode, players can fight for their lives, eating food to keep their hunger up while crafting shelter and gaining experience. Resources are finite and must be collected before they can be used to make anything. You can (and will) die, or kill other players in survival mode.

Creative mode is a bit different from survival mode in Minecraft PE. For starters, there are no limits on the resources available to you – everything can be pulled from an in game menu and put into your inventory, to be used an infinite number of times. There are no enemies and they don't spawn, so you don't have to worry about Creepers crawling up behind you and ruining your day.

Survival mode is for those players who want a thrill while playing Minecraft PE. Being able to die makes living that much more exciting, and all that. Creative mode is perfect for people who want to, well, create something. Massive mansions or expansive skyscrapers take lots of time and resources to build in survival mode. With all points considered, these two different modes are really like two completely different games. Try them both out and see for yourself.

T EMPLES

Temples are structures which have a chance of being randomly generated when a new world is created. They can appear in deserts, where they are made of sandstone and various wool types, or in jungles, where they are made from tons of cobblestone. The differences between these temples are more than just cosmetic though, running quite a bit deeper in reality.

Jungle temples feature dispensers, tripwires and arrow traps ready to fill an unwary player full of extra holes. They feature a single, easy to find chest, along with a hidden room which contains several boxes of treasure. Players are encouraged to try and figure out how to open the secret door with the trio of nearby levers, rather than just breaking down the wall with a pick. Both methods get you to the goods on the other side, though.

Desert temples feature pressure plates and TNT, which make an effective and deadly trap when paired together. At the bottom level of every desert temple, there is a design etched into the floor, made from orange and blue wool. By removing this wool, a path down a long drop will be revealed, along with the four treasure chests at the bottom. These generally come loaded with bones, iron, gold, diamonds and food. If you're careful, you can grab 9 blocks of TNT to take back home with you too.

Temples are dark inside and usually loaded with enemies, so it's not a good idea to just go waltzing into one. Make sure you have some armor and a decent weapon handy if you don't want that nice temple you found to become a tomb for you.

Under the Water

Water in Minecraft PE is both helpful and hazardous, being a useful tool and something which will kill you just the same. It can be used to put out fires, quickly clear land and help crops grow faster by improving cultivated land nearby. There is relatively little to be found at the bottom of the ocean and under the water, though.

In the PC and Xbox versions of Minecraft, fishing and boating are both implemented and allow for much interaction between the player and large bodies of water. As for Minecraft PE, the game is still waiting for a few patches to bring it up to pace. This means, for now anyhow, that there isn't much reason at all to go diving or exploring under the ocean.

If you regularly enjoy Minecraft PE with other people, building a home beneath the water could prove a great way to keep other people out, or stop them from ever finding your residence in the first place. Drowning is a real possibility when living underwater, but there are *no* monsters which spawn in the ocean, so dangers outside of the environment are minimal.

Villages

Villages, like temples, are randomly generated at the time a world is created. They contain a handful of villagers, sometimes a blacksmith, always a slew of farm plots which prove an excellent source of seeds, wheat, potatoes and carrots. They make great places to set up your home if you don't have a house already when you happen to find them.

Villagers are a great way to get your hands on some unique items, as well as things you couldn't possibly create with the resources you have available. Villagers will always be looking to trade something they have for something you have, but every villager has a different deal in mind. Some will want food, others will want resources. In many cases, you will be able to find the items villagers are asking for in the very same village where they're standing.

Mobs will attack NPC villages and kill the people living there without prejudice, so if you do decide to move into a village, you will need to shore it up against invaders. A simple fence around the perimeter will be enough to keep bad things from getting in – or your villagers from getting out. Villagers who are attacked will flee for their lives, sometimes running off in a direction until they're just a dot on the horizon, then gone altogether.

By replacing the doors on homes with solid blocks, you can keep villagers locked in their houses and keep enemies locked out. This will be enough to stop creepers from blowing up houses if you put the block in the upper space where the door was. This will cut off the line of sight for monsters outside the home and keep the villagers inside safe.

Weather in Minecraft PE comes down to a few simple options. Either there is rain or there isn't rain. In colder places, the rain becomes snow and has a different graphic, but it is still just rain all the same. Weather has very little effect on the world around you in this game, which is to say it is mostly negligible, except for one key point.

In areas where snowfall regularly occurs, water will freeze over and turn into ice. This is bad news for people trying to farm that land, because their water will continually freeze up unless they do something about it. Keeping lit torches near water sources will stop them from freezing over, but that's not always an option, especially for those low on coal.

The above is not true for areas that have snow on the ground. That is not an effective marker for which land is good or bad to build upon. Only places where snow regularly falls will feature this effect, so it might be best to avoid those particular biomes completely.

During heavy storms and rainfall, it is possible to go to sleep and skip through the duration of the event, to the next day. This is just like sleeping at night, except you can do it anytime during the storm. Besides these two points, the weather in Minecraft PE has very little effect on the game.

Xtra Features

Just like the PC version of Minecraft, there are many mods available to download for Minecraft PE. Mods exist which provide infinite health, super jumps, limitless items and other great advantages. Finding, downloading and installing these mods is to be done at the player's own risk.

Because the websites where mods such as these are stored could be operated by literally anybody, be careful about where you go to get your xtra features. Established, respected websites do exist and can be found with enough searching, but it's impossible to just come out and recommend any particular one. You never know when something is going to go bad with a favorite website, after all.

Yummy Stuff

Food is an important part of Minecraft PE for those who are playing on survival mode. Players must eat regularly or suffer from starvation's effects, which are enough to bring them to half health, or right to the brink of death on higher difficulties. Food is available just about everywhere and can be found, or made, with a little effort on your part.

Most animals drop meat which can either be eaten raw or cooked. Cooked food restores more hunger and saturation points than uncooked food. Some raw foods, like chicken, can actually make the player sick and cause illness for a period of time. Most foods should be cooked as a rule, but sometimes there's no furnace nearby to get the job done.

Thankfully, there are foods which can be prepared right in your inventory. If you have a wooden bowl handy, combining two different mushrooms will yield a soup which is quite satisfying. The empty bowl will remain after eating this, so it can used to create multiple bowls of soup with multiple mushrooms.

Saturation is a hidden meter which keeps track of how good the last piece of food you ate was. Better foods, like steaks, keep you feeling fuller for longer, giving you more saturation points. Light foods like cookies or bread may fill you up eventually, but you will burn through that hunger meter quickly because the food has a low saturation value.

Zones

The world of Minecraft PE is made up of several different zones, or biomes. These present different places to live, with different living conditions in each. There are mountains and hills, oceans and islands, deserts, plains and jungles to find in the typical Minecraft PE world. Each of these present circumstances unique from one another.

Mountains are tall and wide, often full of ore and standing well above ground level. They can take a lot of effort to climb, but building up high is never a bad idea. Ladders make ascending mountains much easier, but jumping up and placing blocks just under yourself always works for getting to the top too.

Deserts are full of sand and very little water. No animals spawn naturally in the desert, so finding food can be a bit of a problem. It's also impossible to grow anything in all that sand, except for sugar canes, so you will have to bring in dirt from elsewhere if you want to make a living. Deserts have the occasional desert temple, which might make a good place to set up your home.

Jungles are full of trees and difficult to navigate because of all the growth. They also feature temples like the deserts, which are actually a bit different in size and shape. Jungles feature all kinds of animals and chickens, cows, sheep and pigs will all spawn in jungle biomes. They have a wide variety of life but are difficult to maneuver.

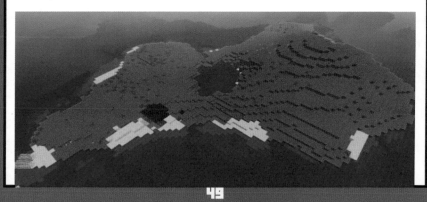

MY MINECRAFT:

THE NAME OF MY WORLDS

_____

_____

_____

_____

_____

_____

_____

_____

_____

_____

TIPS I WANT TO REMEMBER: